T0146707

WHY GOD
DID NOT
MAKE
ANYONE
Homosexual

WHY GOD DID NOT MAKE ANYONE
Homosexual

RON SEARCY

iUniverse®

WHY GOD DID NOT MAKE ANYONE HOMOSEXUAL

The Holy Bible, English Standard Version (ESV) is adapted from the Revised Standard Version of the Bible, copyright Division of Christian Education of the National Council of the Churches of Christ in the U.S.A. All rights reserved.

iUniverse books may be ordered through booksellers or by contacting:

iUniverse
1663 Liberty Drive
Bloomington, IN 47403
www.iuniverse.com
1-800-Authors (1-800-288-4677)

Because of the dynamic nature of the Internet, any web addresses or links contained in this book may have changed since publication and may no longer be valid. The views expressed in this work are solely those of the author and do not necessarily reflect the views of the publisher, and the publisher hereby disclaims any responsibility for them.

Any people depicted in stock imagery provided by Thinkstock are models, and such images are being used for illustrative purposes only. Certain stock imagery © Thinkstock.

ISBN: 978-1-5320-0208-3 (sc)
ISBN: 978-1-5320-0207-6 (e)

Print information available on the last page.

iUniverse rev. date: 07/18/2016

Preface

As I write this book in 2014, so far, there have been nineteen (19) states that have had their anti- homosexual marriage laws struck down by federal courts. This is in spite of the United States Supreme Court ruling in 1986 in the case of Bowers Verses Hardwick that upheld the right of states to make homosexual activity a crime.

So far, twenty nine states have passed laws allowing homosexuals to marry their own gender. Why? Like most people, our lawmakers are totally ignorant of what God has to say about the matter because very few actually study the bible. Oh, a few read it, many listen to their minister or, Sunday school teacher but, hardly any actually studies the bible. God says to study to show you are approved to him, not just read.

If one did study, you would see that God not only compares homosexuality to having sex with your own mother, he says that those who support homosexuality, is worthy of death. I have listed those scriptures in this book so, you can read for yourself.

I once attended a public meeting when Al Gore was a US Senator and clearly recall him saying the minority runs this country because they make the most noise. They get organized, get the media's attention and sell their agenda to the general public. Homosexuals have tried to say they have the same right to marry their own gender, no different than a man and a woman marrying. That argument didn't get very far with the Supreme Court.

I hope I have your attention enough to read this book and learn the real truth about homosexuality.

Dedication

I dedicate this book to my best friend and fellow Christian, Janie. By accident, eighteen (18) years ago as I write this, God surely put us together.

Many pretend to be friends or, are friends until money is thrown in and sadly, you find out that the person you thought you could trust, isn't the person you thought. It's rare to find a real friend who will be there when you need them and you can totally trust them and laugh all the time. Janie is that kind of person and I value her friendship so much and want her to know because of who and what she is, is why I love her so much.

Memorial

To my daughter, Pamela Lynn Searcy Doster, July 5, 1969 - July 14, 2014. Murdered in Tampa, Florida. As with your sister that proceeded you in death by cancer, Pammie, your dad loved you and your sister, Rhonda, so very much. I will see you both in heaven soon.

Acknowledgment

I couldn't finish this book without acknowledging the help Mrs. Kirsten Guzman has given me in typing this book and my previous book, "From Bankruptcy To A Millionaire - Twice: A True Story. Kirsten, I appreciate you so much.

Contents

Chapter 1

How Someone Can Really Believe a Lie

First, in a study, or debate, on the subject of morality there has to be a basis of authority which, of course, is the bible. Morality has to do with the mindset of a person. One either chooses to do good or evil. One isn't born to be a fornicator and cheat on their mate, it's something they choose to do. In most cases of cheating in a marriage, the cheater didn't just decide they were going to cheat, it's because they either allowed evil to overcome them or, they fed their minds with porn. Your mind is sort of like a computer, what comes out is dependent on what you put in it.

Before I deal with what God has to say about homosexuality, whether or not homosexuals were born that way or not, you must first understand about the sub-conscience mind and how it works in your life and how easy it is to brain wash another person. People who watch porn don't even realize that slowly, but surely, it warps their minds and makes them into perverts, not even realizing what porn has done to them and even thinking it doesn't affect them to watch it.

If you think you aren't brainwashed then, let me ask you a few questions and see if you are, or not. Someone once said, if you don't use your mind, someone else will. Few of us challenge what we have been taught. When you finished school and your mom and dad banked at a certain bank, I bet I can tell you where you bank. If, in a religion, if your mom and dad attended a certain church, I bet I can tell you where you attend. If mom and dad has their car insurance with a certain company, I bet I can tell you where you have yours. Still think you aren't brainwashed? Drugs and porn are somewhat alike. Nearly every person you will meet who is doing hard drugs, started with weed and/ or, drinking and as time went by, they slowly progressed deeper and deeper until the drugs and/or pills ruled their lives.

Porn is the same way. One starts off looking at porn and it slowly warps their minds and they keep trying different things and finally get to the point of swingers, swapping mates, bestiality and all kinds of perverted sexual things. I have seen it happen several times. I used to have a branch manager who was a great guy, early 40's and had a great wife. He started looking at porn and went from the national average of sex twice a week at his age, to ten times a day. What? Folks, that came from his wife's own mouth. He had to seek professional help. What has this to do with homosexuality? Plenty. One can do wrong and not even realize it until they are hooked and in most cases, already ruined their marriage and their life.

Before I bore you and lose your attention, I am trying to show you how someone can believe something with all their might yet, can be a total falsehood. It all starts with the mind in how we act, how we think and the choices we make.

King Soloman, the wisest man to ever live said: "For as a man thinks in his mind, so is he." Proverbs 23:7. Jesus, in Matthew 15:17-20 said, "Do you not yet understand that whatever enters the mouth goes into the stomach and is eliminated? But those things that proceed out of the mouth come from the mind and these defile a man. For out of the mind proceeds evil thoughts, murders, adulteries, fornications, thefts, false witness, blasphemies. These are the things that defile a man, not eating with unwashed hands. That doesn't defile a man. Our minds are developed by what we see, what we are taught, by the influence of those around us and by what we hear. Lack of Godly training, hanging out with evil minded persons and such generally ends up with that person in jail and a blight on society.

Were the Muslim fanatics that want to kill us all, born that way? Of course not. They are that way because of how they were raised, by what they saw in films or, literature, the influence of family, friends and/or religious leaders they trust. Do they believe with all their heart that it's Gods will that they eliminate all non Muslims? You better believe they believe it. They are willing to blow themselves up for their belief yet, the rest of the world can easily see how messed up in the head they really are. They are taught to believe that if they die for their cause, they will go to Heaven and have seven (7) virgins. Dumb, dumb, dumb. Where in the Bible or, Koran does it teach any such nonsense. It doesn't. Were men who want their own daughter born that way? Of course not. Was any man born to want some woman to dress up in leather with a whip, call them degrading names and inflict pain on them during sex, born that way? Of course not. Was any man born to want sex with a ten (10) year old? Of course not. All these things that are unnatural were learned how be it, they weren't aware of what they were feeding into their minds, caused them to be that way.

Time is also a major factor. For instance, when I was a teenager, the first movie that showed a woman in her slip was, *Cat On A Hot Tin Roof*, starring Elizabeth Taylor. I recall very well the national and local reaction. The religious leaders were all torn up along with millions of people who thought it was a national disgrace. Back then, when women sat down, they made sure their knees were covered. There was, with few exceptions, no such thing as having sex with a woman who wasn't married. Though today, it is still fornication, no one thinks anything about it because, almost all do it. Look at the movies today that are available to our kids to see. You see, over a long period of time, people accept evil because it's fun.

This is exactly what homosexuals have done to you and you not even realize it. They are friends, relatives, co-workers, etc. and they sound so sincere on really believing they were born that way. As you will soon see, God says it's not natural. "For this reason, God gave them up to disgusting passions. For even their women exchanged the natural use of their bodies for what is against nature. Likewise the men, leaving the natural use of the woman's body burned in their lust for one another, men with men, committing shameful sexual acts and receiving in themselves the penalty of their error which was due and given as they did not want to retain God in their knowledge, God gave them over to a degraded mind to do those things which are not natural being filled with all unrighteousness, sexual immorality, wickedness, covetousness, maliciousness, full of envy, murder, strife, deceit, evil mindedness, they are whisperers, back biters, haters of God, violent, proud, boasters, inventors of evil things, disobedient to parents, undiscerning, untrustworthy, unloving, unforgiving, unmerciful, who, knowing the righteous judgment of God that those who practice such things, are worthy of death and also those who approve of those who practice such things." ROMANS 1: 26-32.

I want to show you how millions of people can be lead to believe a lie so, you can understand what homosexuals have done to millions in their thinking.

In America, we are lead to believe, go to college and you will be successful. If I told you that other than the high end paying positions such as, a doctor, dentist, engineer, etc., going to college was a total waste of time and money, you would says I am nuts. I can prove what I say very easily. The US Census Bureau says that sixty-seven percent (67%) of all Americans age sixty-five (65) and older retire in poverty. That figure includes those with a college degree. Now, instead of going to college and being broke at age sixty-five(65), let's say you took the same amount of money it takes to get a degree, let's say, one hundred thousand dollars ($100,000) and put it in even a poor performing bond and only got three percent(3%), at age 65, you would have over eight hundred thousand dollars($800,000) in the bank. Still think going to college works? In fact, most of the people I have known over the years who have a degree, don't even work in the field they studied. They spend one hundred thousand dollars ($100,000) and wind up working as a clerk or, some warehouse in shipping. In going to college, one just lost four (4) prime fun years of their lives. Many of the courses people are required to take have absolutely nothing to do with their chosen field.

The one hundred thousand dollars ($100,000) isn't the real cost because one has to also include the one hundred thousand dollars they could have made had they not gone to college. Now, when one gets a degree, they will average fifteen thousand dollars ($15,000) a year more income than those without a degree so, it will take them to age thirty eight (38) just to get even.

Pick any town or, city you wish and look at how those with a degree versus those without a degree live on a daily level. Both have a house payment, or rent. Both have a car payment. Both have to pay an electric bill, both have to pay a water bill, both have to pay for TV service. Both, on the average, are seven thousand five hundred dollars ($7,500.00) in credit card debt. Both have to fight rush hour traffic twice a day. Both, on the average, hate their boss. Some call this, living life to its fullest. I call that misery. The financial difference between those with a degree and those without? Those with a degree usually have a little nicer car and house but, they also have the higher debt that goes with it.

Unless you want to do like everyone else and keep repeating this lifestyle week after week for the next forty (40) years, you better go into business for yourself, learn a trade or, marry someone who is already financially secure.

This book is about homosexuality however, I can't just leave this without further opening your eyes. I want to say to you, this is America, a free enterprise system which means the only reason that is keeping you from being wealthy is, you. You have accepted working for someone else, being told what to do, living pay check to pay check because that's what almost everyone else does. In larger towns and cities, people just accept that every morning and every evening, they are going to have to spend an hour or two of their time, bumper to bumper, traffic lights, stop signs, etc, etc. You are brainwashed.

You have also been brainwashed into believing it takes a degree and lots of money to start your own business. Bologna. Being in business for yourself isn't easy and it's not for everyone but, for those like me who are dying to be somebody and can't stand working for someone else, there is nothing like it. How does it feel to be wealthy (Income over $100,000 a year)? A thousand times better than you would think. There are all kinds of stories out there where people kept their jobs and started a business part time. We have all read about the woman who made millions with a better chocolate chip cookie.

Where and how in the world would someone really ambitious even start since there is no school that teaches one how to become wealthy? I am going to be down to earth and tell you how I did it with less than four hundred dollars ($400.00) to start and had to go to summer school to get out of high school. I am a common sense person so I got every book I could find written by people who had already made it, to see how they did it. I started at age 24. By age 33, I was a self made millionaire. If I can do it, so can anyone else. I won't take up any more space here about what I did. You can read about it in my book, From Bankruptcy To A Millionaire - Twice: A true story.

One of the best examples of being brain washed is, by the religious world. Several years ago, a cult leader in Waco, TX convinced normally intelligent moms and dads that it was Gods will that they give him their thirteen year old daughter for sex and he convinced more than one set of parents. How did this pervert do such a thing? Remember, if you don't use your mind, someone else will. Like most, they didn't know the bible well enough to refute him.

Over the ages, men have complained about their wives fussing at them and it continues today as the number one thing men complain about when talking about their wife. Granted ladies, most husbands get fussed at by you because they aren't doing what they should do as a husband. Anyway, using religion is the best way to control women. Just look at the Muslim world and how they do it. The wife has to jump every time the husband says frog. Otherwise, she will be subject to a beating. Let a man rape a woman in their world and she is looked upon as having done something wrong. Their leader, Muhammad, also had a thirteen year old wife. So did Joseph Smith that started the Mormon church, and he had more than one wife. Joseph Smith claimed to have received a golden plaque that Jesus gave him that had an updated version of the bible called, The Book of Mormon. He claimed to have two witnesses that saw it but, somehow, it got lost. The people from the Church of Christ pointed out several flaws in the Book of Mormon so, the Mormons removed those flaws and re-printed the Book of Mormon. So much for his so called golden plaque. Their doctrine has fooled millions.

How did Jim Jones convince hundreds of normally intelligent people to quit their jobs and give their worldly possessions to him, leave their relatives and relocate half way around the world to a jungle and start over in the middle of nowhere? How did he get over two hundred people to all take poison and kill themselves? He did it by brainwashing them and playing their emotions to that it was God's will. He used the fact that most people depend on their preacher to get guidance and only a few actually study for themselves therefore they subject themselves to his opinion of what the bible says.

Fifty (50) years ago, if a person practiced homosexuality, it was viewed, as it rightfully should, a sexual prevision. Do you now see how, over a period of time and lack of your own biblical knowledge, homosexuals have used your mind and why most just don't think much about it? Homosexuals claim that they just want what's fair and have equality. Millions have bought this idea since it seems fair. No, no, no. They have no right to equality because they are doing something they shouldn't do begin with that is definitely a sexual perversion. As you will soon see, God has always viewed homosexuality as, extremely disgusting. So should you.

When I stop and think about what a sexual pervert is doing to a little girl, it's extremely disgusting to me. Same with a father that wants sex with his own daughter. How could any father even have such a thought? I may find another man good looking but, that doesn't mean I should go after him and want sex with another man. In case some of you people haven't figured it out on your own, the mouth was naturally intended for chewing food, tasting food, talking and kissing. The rectum is for passing human food waste. The next time you decide to put another man's penis in your mouth, ask yourself when was the last time the other guy washed since the last time he urinated? Before you lick on another woman's private parts, ask yourself the same question. That's nasty. UGH.

Was anybody born a thief? Was anyone born a fornicator? Was anyone born to murder someone else? Was any man born to beat on his wife, or other women? No, these sins were learned by various ways and more importantly, they all are a choice a person makes. Four year old little Johnny watches ole dad come home from work, plop his butt in his easy chair and yells at mom to bring him a beer. Mom says she is busy helping with the kids' homework. Dad gets angry because he can't control her so, he beats on her. Mom has to help dad make a living but, unlike Dad, when she comes home, she has to fix dinner, clean up the table, wash dishes, help the kids with homework, clean the house, wash clothes, etc, etc. No wonder she doesn't feel like sex physically at bed time but, she does just so she won't get beaten again. Guess how little Johnny thinks a husband should act when he gets married? Ole dad cheats on her but she now has two kids, he probably will refuse to pay child support. She doesn't make enough to support herself and the kids. She isn't about to give up her kids so, she is stuck with him and the continued beatings when she doesn't do what he wants. He really loves her, doesn't he?

Do you now see how, over time, one develops their thinking and how their thinking changes their actions? There is not one set answer why someone becomes a homosexual. I really don't know how much influence this has to do with being one but, I personally have seen boys turn homosexual in cases where their dad was mean to them. In one case, the three (3) sons all turned homosexual and the one daughter turned out straight. The daughter was treated totally different that the boys were. Another case where acceptance of homosexuality occurs is, a lady goes to a night club and sees another hot chic kissing on another one and it looks like they are having fun so, one night while drinking heavy, she decides to try it. This is the same way people get hooked on drugs, pills, and booze, someone they trusted, told them to try it and they did.

As I point out often, very few people actually study the bible and that includes many that claim to be Christians. Oh sure, they may attend services and get to listen to their preacher or, Sunday school teacher and some read their bible daily. All that's good but, when one doesn't actually study then, they leave themselves open to someone else using their mind, similar to what I showed you about getting a college education.

In my own case, my dad wouldn't allow mom to attend any religious services. He never went one time. As I pointed out, God has always drawn me to him so, I went with a neighbor and was raised as a Baptists. Naturally, I believed what Baptists believe, doctrinal wise. One of the biggest issues was, Baptists, in general, do not believe water baptism is necessary to be saved.

One day when I was in my early twenties, I met the most unusual man I had ever met. His background was a former Baptist. He was now a Minister for another religious group. Over the years, of course, I had many religious groups knock on my door and give me their literature but, this time, this man, I will call Ken, had me studying on my own for the first time in my life. He didn't try to teach me anything about what he believed. He had me start with the word, Baptism and using a concordance (one that has every word in the bible and what book and verse where it is located), I looked up every passage in the New Testament that had the words, Baptize or, baptism. It didn't take very long for me to see myself that I had been taught wrong.

I never thought much about other religious groups as, they all had people who believed in God and Jesus but, believed a little different than, my group. I knew enough about the Bible at that point to know about Gods warnings against teaching false doctrine and also about how stern God is about adding to or, taking away from what is written in the Bible. So, now, what do I do?

I first used a Greek Dictionary to look up the words meaning and found that the definition was to, dip, plunge or, immerse. I already knew there were some groups that used "sprinkling" for Baptism so, I concluded that all they get is, wet, they do not get Baptized according to the definition of the word. Sprinkling is a man made false doctrine.

I really didn't intend to get into other doctrinal issues but, at the same time, I can't just leave you wondering what else I did and let you see the impact something so simple had on my life.

In Acts chapter 2, after Peter had preached and had shown most of the crowd that they partook of the killing of Gods son, the crowd had heard the word, had believed what Peter said so, naturally, they asked the question of what should they do next? Peter told them, in verse thirty eight (38) to repent and be Baptized for the remission of their sins. First, the words, and, but and or, are conjunctions connecting two words of equal importance. Next, ask yourself the same question I asked myself, what is the purpose of being Baptized? Peter tells us there. He said Baptism did away with sins so, the opposite of that is, if one is not Baptized, they must still have their sins.

Since I was raised as a Baptists, I know what they will say and that is, Jesus said, "Believe on the Lord Jesus Christ and you will be saved." That statement is true however, is there more to just believing? The scripture says the devils believe also and tremble so, believing alone won't cut it. In Romans chapter seven (7), Women are told they are bound to their husbands for life, no matter what. In 1 Corinthians chapter 11, there is an exception to women being bound and that is, if her husband leaves her, she is no longer bound or, if he dies. One has to, "rightfully divide the word of truth." To just use, "Believe on the Lord Jesus Christ and you will be saved" is taken totally out of context.

In Mark 16: 15-16, Jesus said, "He that believes and is Baptized shall be saved." See, there is more to just believing. Again, the use of the word, "and", connects two words of equal importance. The opposite of what Jesus had to say is, he that don't, won't. In Galatians chapter three (3), verses 26 and 27, Paul explains why one should be Baptized. One is Baptized into Christ. It is symbolic of the death, burial and resurrection of Jesus. Just as Jesus died and was buried so, likewise, we as Christians are buried in a watery grave and raised to walk in newest of life because, being Baptized, washes away our sins so, we are a new creature in Christ. If one isn't in Christ then, they must be out and the only way to get into Christ is to be Baptized into him. The only way to rid ourselves of the old man (woman) of sin is through Baptism.

One day, I thought, this Church says they are right, that church says they are right, on and on and on so, which one really is the one you read about in the New Testament? The first thing would be if any today's Churches matched the Bibles blueprint of organization. In 1 Timothy and Titus, the Bible clearly sets out that a group of men called, Elders and to lead the congregation and under them are a group of men called Deacons. If you attend any so called church that is not organized like this, you better get out as fast as you can as, it is a false church. To have one man run a certain congregation is, false doctrine.

For any leader to wear special clothing and elevate themselves above the rest of that congregation is, going beyond biblical teaching and is also false doctrine. The first century church met on the first day of the week (Sunday). They partook of the Lords Supper every Sunday. Though they had instruments, they did not use them. They weren't brought into a religious service for over 1,700 years after Christ and that was by the Catholics. Common sense, someone had to teach them God doesn't want instruments in worship to him. Why? I don't have a clue but, I do know we are all warned to not add anything to what he has written. To baptize a baby is, false doctrine. Baptism is for the remission of sins and a baby has no sin. To teach someone else they can't marry because of religious reasons, is another man made doctrine and so is teaching that a Christian can't eat certain things on a certain day. There is no biblical authority for any person to call themselves a Pope or a Cardinal or, any other name other than what God has authorized. See now why one needs to seek Gods truths for themselves?

NOTES

NOTES

NOTES

NOTES

Chapter 2

What God Has to Say about Homosexuality

Genesis 9:18-28 "Now, the sons of Noah who went out of the ark were, Shem, Ham and Japheth. And Ham was the father of Canaan. These three were the sons of Noah and from these the whole earth was populated. Noah began to be a farmer and he planted a vineyard. He then drank some of the wine and was drunk and became uncovered in his tent I want to make a note here that many scholars believe it had never rained on the earth until the great flood and that is why the people made fun of Noah and why he preached for over one hundred (100) years and never converted anyone but, his own family. They believe the earth was like a green house therefore, grapes would only produce grape juice and would not ferment so, no one ever got drunk from drinking grape juice, it wasn't wine but, after the flood, it did rain and the green house effect was removed so, Noah, not realizing this, had made wine and drank it, thinking it was just grape juice.

Verse 21: "Then he drank of the wine and was drunk and became uncovered in his tent. And Ham, the father of Canaan, saw the nakedness of his father and told his two brothers outside. But Shem and Japheth took a garment, laid it on both their shoulders and went backward and covered the nakedness of their father. Their faces were turned away and they did not see their father's nakedness. So, Noah awoke from his wine and knew what his younger son had done to him. Then he said, "cursed be Canaan, a servant of servants. He shall be to his brothers. And he said, "Blessed be the Lord, The God of Shem and may Canaan be his servant. May God enlarge Japheth and may he dwell in the tents of Shem and may Canaan be his servant."

I don't have a clue why homosexuals want to bring this passage up. It proves nothing, one way or, the other. They want it to say that Ham performed oral sex on his father while Noah was drunk. Where does it say that? Maybe Noah realized Ham had seen him naked and not tried to cover him up, who knows? Seems to me if Ham was going to do that then, why did he even tell his brothers that could then easily catch him? Folks, whether Ham did or didn't, cannot ever be proven either way. Speak where the Bible speaks and be silent where the Bible is silent. At the worst, Ham did perform oral sex on his father. What would he get out of that? The worst is, Ham sinned but, this sure doesn't show anything good about it since, whatever Ham did, he got cursed for it. There is nothing good or, bad for homosexuals here, it's meaningless.

GENESIS 19: 1 - 29 is the story of the sinful cities of Sodom and Gomorrah. Lot was a righteous man, living in Sodom. Lot was the son of Abraham's brother (Genesis 14: 12) Two angels came to Lot to let him know that God was going to destroy Sodom and to get himself and his family out promptly. The bible doesn't say if the angels were extremely good looking and is why many men of the city came to lots door, asking Lot to send them out. Homosexuality isn't specifically mentioned but, it's hard to believe the men of the city wanted to play marbles with them as, Lot offered the men his two daughters. The bible doesn't say Sodom and Gomorrah were destroyed because of homosexuality. In fact, in EZEKIEL 16: 49 It claims the sins of Sodom were pride, gluttony, sloth, greed, and failure to help the poor. However, we can know homosexuality was a big part of the destruction because afterward, the bible refers to homosexuals as, Sodomites and sometimes, dogs as you will see later.

LEVITICUS 18:22

You shall not lie (have sex with) a man as with a woman. It is an abomination. NOTE: Abomination means, "extremely disgusting."

LEVITICUS 20: 13

If a man lies with a man as he lies with a woman, both of them have committed an extremely disgusting act. Kill them both. Their blood shall be upon them. NOTE: A man who has sex with his own mother (or step mother) or, his daughter-in-law is in the same sexual perverted category as a homosexual. Is it natural for a man to want sex with his own mother. Is it natural for any man to want sex with his own daughter-in-law? Of course not. They weren't born to want that, they became mentally perverted. Disgusting thought. Then, what makes you think that any man who would want another man sexually, is natural? A man who rather have his penis in the rear of another man than he had in a woman's vagina? Come on, that's sick.

LEVITICUS: 20 11-12

The man who lies with his father's wife has uncovered his nakedness: both of them shall surely be put to death. Their blood shall be upon them. If a man lies with his daughter-in-law, both of them shall surely be put to death. They have committed a perversion. Their blood shall be upon them. NOTE: God finds homosexuality such a disgusting sexual perversion that it warrants capital punishment.

NOTE: Since it is impossible for homosexuals to use the bible to uphold their sexual perversion then, attacking it is what they do. I just covered scripture from the Old Testament that was part of Moses law. Homosexuals are correct in that Moses law was given to the nation of Israel only. Actually, what I quoted was part of Moses law. Most people think in the terms of the Ten Commandments but, there were actually six hundred thirteen (613) commandments given to the nation of Israel.

Homosexuals say these laws do not apply to them because gentiles had no law. Many today thinks that the Ten Commandments applies to the way one should live. WRONG. "The Lord made not this covenant with our fathers, but with us, even us (Jews or, children of Israel) who are all of us here alive this day."

DEUTERONOMY 5:3.

The law of Moses was given about 1450 BC.

Are we to believe just because thousands of years have passed that God has changed his mind about sins? He still views murder, rape, incest, lying, stealing, fornication, homosexuality and such as things that are sinful and if one practices them, will definitely not make it to heaven as we will see when we start looking at what the new Testament has to say about homosexuality.

ROMANS 1: 26 – 28

For this reason God gave them up to vile passions. For even their women (Lesbians) exchanged the natural use for what is against nature. Likewise also the men leaving the natural use of the woman burned in their lust for one another, men with men committing what is shameful, and receiving in themselves the penalty of their error which was due. NOTE: God says it's not natural for someone to be with another of their kind so, there are two choices here. You can believe homosexuals when they claim they were born that way or, you can believe God. No middle ground. Since it's impossible for God to lie, I believe I will stick with God. Did you notice that God said here that homosexuality was lust?

ROMANS 1: 31 - 32

Undiscerning, untrustworthy, unloving, unforgiving, unmerciful who knowing the righteous judgment of God, that those who practice such things are deserving of death, not only do the same but also approve of those who practice them.

NOTE: Lawmakers, many of you have been brainwashed by homosexuals by their love and equality line of lies and are in a heap of trouble, come the day of judgment by passing such ungodly laws on same sex marriage and equality laws. The bible (if you read this book and read the verses I have listed) clearly says homosexuality is not natural and God finds it so disgusting that he put homosexuals in the same perverted category as any man who would want sex with his own mother or, a daughter - in - law. He says here that those who support homosexuals are just as bad and are worthy of death. You need a head exam if you see nothing unnatural, nothing disgusting with one man with another man's penis in his mouth or, one man's penis in the rectum of another man. You are as sick in the head as they are if that's ok with you.

1 CORINTHIANS 6: 9 - 10

Do you not know that the unrighteous will not inherit the kingdom of God? Do not be deceived, neither fornicators, nor idolaters, nor adulterers, nor homosexuals, nor sodomites, nor thieves, nor covetous, nor drunkards, nor revilers, nor extortionist will inherit the kingdom of God.

1 TIMOTHY 1: 8 - 10

But we know that the law is good if one uses it lawfully. Knowing this that the law is not made for a righteous person, but for the lawless and insubordinate, for the ungodly and for sinners, for the unholy and profane, for murderers of fathers and murderers of mothers, for manslayers, for fornicators, for sodomites (homosexuals), for kidnappers, for liars, for perjures, and if there be any other thing that is contrary to sound doctrine.

2 TIMOTHY 3: 1 - 5

But know this, that in the last days perilous times will come, for men will be lovers of themselves, lovers of money, boasters, proud, blasphemers, disobedient to parents, unthankful, unholy, unloving, unforgiving, slanderers, without natural affection (homosexuals), brutal, despisers of good, traitors, headstrong, haughty, lovers of pleasure rather than lovers of God having a form of godliness but denying its power. And from such people turn away.

JUDE: 7 - 8

As Sodom and Gomerrah and the cities around them in a similar manner to these, having given themselves over to sexual immorality and gone after strange flesh (homosexuals), are set forth as an example, suffering the vengeance of eternal fire. Likewise also these dreamers defile the flesh, reject authority, and speak evil of dignitaries.

REVELATION 22: 14 - 15

Blessed are those who do His commandments, that they may have the right to the tree of life, and may enter through the gates into the city but outside are dogs (HOMOSEXUALS) and sorcerers and sexually immoral and murderers and whoever loves and practices a lie.

NOTES

NOTES

NOTES

NOTES

Chapter 3

Biblical Marriage

GENESIS 1:26-28

Then God said, "Let US make man in OUR image, according to OUR likeness; let them have dominion over the fish of the sea, over the birds of the air and over the cattle; over all the earth and over every creature and over every creeping thing that creeps on the earth. So God created man in his own image; in the image of God HE created him; male and female HE created them. And God blessed them. And God said to them, "Be fruitful and multiply and fill the earth and subdue it and have dominion over the fish of the sea and over the birds of the heavens and over every living thing that moves on the earth.

GENESIS 2:7

And the Lord God formed man of the dust of the ground and breathed into his nostrils the breath of life and man became a living being

GENESIS 2: 18-25

Then the Lord God said, "it is not good that the man should be alone; I will make him a helper fit for him." Now, out of the ground the Lord God had formed every beast of the field and every bird of the heavens and brought them to the man to see what he would call them. And whatever the man called every living creature, that was it's name. The man gave names to all livestock and to the birds of the air and to every beast of the field. But, for Adam there was not found a helper fit for him. So, the Lord God caused a deep sleep to fall upon the man, and while he slept took one of his ribs and closed up its place with flesh. And the rib that the Lord God had taken from the man he made into a woman and brought her to the man. Then the man said, "This at last is bone of my bones and flesh of my flesh; she shall be called Woman, because she was taken out of man. "Therefore a man shall leave his father and his mother and hold fast to his wife, and they shall become one flesh."

NOTE: In the passages covered so far, notice that a woman was referred to as a man's wife. For any man to call another man his wife is, perverted and disgusting and they have nature out of place. Same goes for any woman who would call a female companion their wife. Your mate is supposed to be a male and a males mate is suppose to be a woman. Women, can you easily see the whole purpose of you being created is to be a companion to your husband, provide sex for him, have children, take care of both and be in charge of the household chores. Also, did you note that a male and a female of each kind of beast, birds, etc is the natural way God set things up. I have been around wild animals and farm animals all my life and not one time did any male have a problem figuring out where his penis naturally belongs. They went for the female vagina every time. Even dumb animals know the rectum is for passing waste, not a sex organ.

GENESIS 11: 29

Then Abram and Nahor took wives. The name of Abram's wife was Sarai, and the name of Nahor's wife, Milcah, the daughter of haran the father of Milcah and Iscah.

NOTE: Again, the mate of a male was a female and a wife is a female.

GENESIS 20: 3

But God came to Abimelech in a dream by night and said to him, "Behold, you are a dead man because of the woman whom you have taken, for she is a mans wife."

NOTE: This is where Abraham pretended that his wife, Sarah, was his sister and Abimelech wasn't aware of it.

GENESIS 20: 9 - 16:

Then Abimelech called Abraham and said to him, "What have you done to us? And how have I sinned against you, that you have brought on me and my kingdom a great sin? You have done to me things that ought not to be done." And Abimelech said to Abraham, "What did you see, that you did this thing?" Abraham said, "I did it because I thought, There is no fear of God at all in this place, and they will kill me because of my wife. Besides, she is indeed my sister, the daughter of my father though not the daughter of my mother, and she became my wife. And when God caused me to wonder from my fathers house, I said to her, "This is the kindness you must do me: at every place to which we come, say of me, He is my brother."

GENESIS 24: 1 - 5

Now, Abraham was old, well advanced in years. And the Lord had blessed Abraham in all things. And Abraham said to his servant, the oldest of his household, who had charge of all that he had, "Put your hand under my thigh, that I may make you swear by the Lord, the God of heaven and God of the earth, that you will not take a wife for my son from the daughters of the Canaanites, among whom I dwell, but, will go to my country and to my kindred, and take a wife for my son Isaac." The servant said to him, "Perhaps the woman may not be willing to follow me to this land. Must I then take your son back to the land which you came?"

GENESIS 28:2

"Arise, go to Paddan - Aram to the house of Bethuel your mothers father, and take as your wife from there one of the daughters of Laban your mothers brother"

GENESIS 29: 15 - 30

Then Laban said to Jacob, "Because you are my kinsman, should you therefore serve me for nothing? Tell me, what shall your wages be?" Now Laban had two daughters. The name of the older was Leah, and the name of the younger was Rachel. Leah's eyes were weak, but, Rachel was beautiful in form and appearance. Jacob loved Rachel and he said, "I will serve you for seven years for your younger daughter, Rachel." Laban said, "It is better that I give her to you than that I should give her to any other man; stay with me."

GENESIS 34:12

"Ask me for as great a bride price and gifts as you will, and I will give whatever you say to me. Only give me the young woman to be my wife."

GENESIS 38:8

Then Judah said to Onan, "Go in to your brother's wife and perform the duty of a brother - in - law to her, and raise up offspring for your brother."

GENSIS 39: 7 - 12

And after a time his masters wife cast her eyes on Joseph and said, "Lie with me." But, he refused and said to his Masters wife, "Behold, because of me my Master has no concern about anything in the house, and he has put everything that he has in my charge. He is not greater in this house than I am, nor has he kept back anything from me except yourself, because you are his wife. How then can I do this great wickedness and sin against God?" And as she spoke to Joseph day after day, he would not listen to her, to lie beside her or to be with her. But one day, when he went into the house to do his work and none of the men of the house was there in the house that she grabbed his clothing and asked him to lie with her but, Joseph fled outside the house.

EXODUS 22:16

"If a man seduces a virgin who is not betrothed and lies with her, he shall give the bride - price for her and make her his wife."

EXODUS 22:17

"If her father utterly refuses to give her to him, he shall pay money equal to the bride - price for virgins."

EXODUS 34:16

"And you take of their daughters for your sons, and their daughters whore after their gods and make your sons whore after their gods."

LEVITICUS 18: 22

"You shall not lie with a man as with a woman, it is an abomination."

NOTE: This says it all. The word, abomination means, extremely disgusting. That is how God feels about homosexuals. Yes, I am very aware God was talking to the Nation of Israel only here and I fully realize we are not under the law of Moses, never were, only Israel however, no one with any intelligence could say God has changed his mind about homosexuality over the years. We will see he hasn't when we get to the New Testament.

LEVITICUS 20:14

"If a man has sex with a woman and her mother also, it is depravity; he and they shall be burned with fire, that there be no depravity among you."

NOTE: Depravity means, a sexual perversion.

LEVITICUS 21:7

"They shall not marry a prostitute or a woman who has been defiled, neither shall they marry a woman divorced from her husband, for the Priest is holy to his God."

NOTE: A Priest under Moses Law could only marry a virgin.

DEUTERONOMY 17: 17

"And he shall not acquire many wives for himself, least his heart turn away, nor shall he acquire for himself excessive silver and gold."

JUDGES 14:2

Then he came up and told his father and mother, "I saw one of the daughters of the Philistines at Timnah. Now get her for me as my wife."

JUDGES 21:21-23

And watch. If the daughters of Shiloh come out to dance in the dances, then come out of the vineyards and snatch each man his wife from the daughters of Shiloh, and go to the land of Benjamin. And when their fathers or their brothers come to complain to us, we will say to them, "Grant them graciously to us, because we did not take for each man of them his wife in battle, neither did you give them to them, else you would now be guilty." And the people of Benjamin did so and took their wives, according to their number, from the dancers whom they carried off. Then they went and returned to their inheritance and rebuilt the towns and lived in them.

1 SAMUEL 18: 17

Then Saul said to David, "Here is my elder daughter Merab. I will give her to you for a wife. Only be valiant for me and fight the Lords battles." For Saul thought, "Let not my hand be against him, but let the hand of the Philistines be against him."

2 Samuel 3:14

Then David sent messengers to Ish-bosheth, Saul's son, saying, "Give me my wife Michal, for whom I paid the bridal price of a hundred foreskins of the Philistines."

EZRA 9:2

For they have taken some of their daughters to be wives for themselves and for their sons, so that the holy race has mixed itself with the peoples of the lands. And in this faithlessness the hand of the officials and chief men has been foremost."

NEHEMIAH 13: 26 - 27

Did not Solomon king of Israel sin on account of such women? Among the many nations there was no king like him, and he was beloved by his God, and God made him king over all Israel. Nevertheless, foreign women made even him to sin. Shall we then listen to you and do this great evil and act treacherously against our God by marrying foreign women?

ESTER 1: 17

For the queens behavior will be made known to all women, causing them to look at their husbands with contempt, since they will say, "King Ahasuerus commanded Queen Vashti to be brought before him, and she did not come."

ESTER 2: 2-4

Then the kings young men who attended him said, "Let beautiful virgins be sought out for the king. And let the king appoint officers in all the provinces of his kingdom to gather all the beautiful young virgins to the harem in Susa the capital, under custody of hegai, the kings eunuch, who is in charge of the women. Let their cosmetics be given them. And let the young women who pleases the king be queen instead of Vashti." This pleased the king and he did so.

PROVERBS 18:22

He who finds a wife finds a good thing and obtains favor from the Lord.

PROVERBS 19: 14

House and wealth are inherited from fathers, but, a prudent wife is from the Lord.

PROVERBS 21: 9

It is better to live on a roof top than in a house with an argumentative woman.

PROVERBS 22:19

It is better to live in a desert land than in a house with a quarrelsome and fretful woman.

HOSEA 1: 2

When the Lord first spoke through Hosea, the Lord said to Hosea, "Go, take to yourself a wife of whoredom and have children of whoredom, for the land commits great whoredom by forsaking the Lord."

HOSEA 12: 12

Jacob fled to the land of Syria; there Israel served for a wife, and for a wife he guarded sheep.

MALACHI 2: 13-16

And this second thing you do. You cover the Lords alter with tears, with weeping and groaning because he no longer regards the offering or accepts it with favor from your hand. But you say, "Why does he not?" Because the Lord was witness between you and the wife of your youth, to whom you have been faithless, though she is your companion and your wife by covenant. Did he not make them one, with a portion of the Spirit in their union? And what was the one God seeking? Godly offspring? So guard yourselves in your spirit, and let none of you be faithless to the wife of your youth. "For the man who does not love his wife but divorces her, says the Lord, the God of Israel, covers his garment with violence, says the Lord of hosts. So, guard yourselves in your spirit, and do not be faithless."

MATTHEW 5: 31

"It was also said, "Whoever divorces his wife, let him give her a certificate of divorce."

MATTHEW 5:32

But I say to you that everyone who divorces his wife, except on the ground of fornication, makes her commit adultery, and if anyone marries a divorced woman commits adultery.

MATTHEW 19: 1-12

Now when Jesus had finished these sayings, he went away from Galilee and entered the region of Jordan. And Pharisees came up to him and tested him by asking, "Is it lawful to divorce ones wife for any cause?" He answered, "Have you not read that he who created them from the beginning made them male and female, and said, "Therefore a man shall leave his father and his mother and hold fast to his wife, and the two shall become one flesh?

NOTE: It says a man and a woman shall become one flesh. Pure and simple, any man who wants to be with another man or, any woman who wants to be with another woman sexually, is all messed up in the head. They are plain perverted and going against nature.

MATTHEW 22: 24

Saying, "Teacher, Moses said, "if a man dies having no children, his brother must marry the widow and raise up children for his brother."

MATTHEW 22: 30

For in the resurrection they neither marry nor are given in marriage, but are like angels in heaven.

MARK 6:17

For it was Herod who had sent and seized John and bound him in prison for the sake of his brother Philips wife, Herodias because Herod had married her.

MARK 10: 2 - 12

And Pharisees came up and in order to test him asked, "Is it lawful for a man to divorce his wife?" He answered them, "What did Moses command you?" They said, "Moses allowed a man to write a certificate of divorce and to send her away." And Jesus said to them, "Because of your hardness of heart he wrote you this commandment. But from the beginning of creation, God made them male and female. "Therefore a man shall leave his father and mother and hold fast to his wife, and the two shall become one flesh, so they are no longer two but one flesh. What therefore God has joined together let no man separate."

MARK 6: 18

For John had been saying to Herod,: It is unlawful for you to have your brothers wife."

MARK 10: 11 - 12

And he said to them, "Whoever divorces his wife and marries another commits adultery against her and if she divorces her husband and marries another, she commits adultery."

MARK 12: 19 -23

"Teacher, Moses wrote for us that if a man's brother dies and leaves a wife, but leaves no child, the man must take the widow and raise up offspring for his brother. There were seven brothers, the first took a wife, and when he died, left no offspring. And the second took her, and died, leaving no offspring. And the third likewise. And the seven left no offspring. Last of all the woman died also. In the resurrection when they rise again, whose wife will she be? For the seven had her as a wife."

MARK 12: 25

For when they rise from the dead, they neither marry nor are given in marriage, but are like angels in heaven.

LUKE 1: 27

To a virgin betrothed to a man whose name was Joseph, of the house of David. And the virgins name was Mary.

LUKE 20:28

And they asked him a question, saying,: Teacher, Moses wrote for us that if a man's brother dies, having a wife but no children the man must take the widow and raise up offspring for his brother.

JOHN 2: 1-5

On the third day there was a wedding at Cana in Galilee, and the mother of Jesus was there. Jesus was also invited to the wedding along with his disciples. When the wine ran out, the mother of Jesus said to him, "They have no wine." And Jesus said to her, "Woman, what does that have to do with me? My hour has not come." His mother said to the servants, "Do whatever he tells you."

LUKE 16: 18

"Everyone who divorces his wife and marries another commits adultery, and he who marries a woman divorced from her husband commits adultery.

ROMANS 7: 1 - 6

Or do you not know, brothers - for I am speaking to those who know the law - that the law is binding on a person only as long as he lives? For a married woman is bound by law to her husband while he lives, but if her husband dies she is released from the law of marriage. Accordingly, she shall be called an adultness if she marries another man while her husband is alive. But if her husband dies, she is free from that law, and if she marries another man she is not an adulteress. Likewise, my brothers, you also have died to the law through the body of Christ, so that you may belong to another, to him who has been raised from the dead, in order that we may bear fruit for God. For while we were living in the flesh, our sinful passions, aroused by the law, were at work in our members to bear fruit for death.

1 CORINTHIANS 6:16

Or do you not know that he who is joined to a prostitute becomes one body with her? For, as it is written, "The two shall become one flesh."

1 CORINTHIANS 7: 1- 40

Now concerning the matters about which you wrote me: "It is good for a man not to have sexual relations with a woman. "But because of the temptation of sexual immorality, each man should have his own wife and each woman her own husband. The husband should give to his wife her conjugal rights, and likewise the wife to her husband. For the wife does not have authority over her own body, but the husband does. Likewise the husband does not have authority over his own body, but the wife does. Do not deprive one another, except perhaps by agreement for a limited time, that you may devote yourselves to prayer, but then come together again, so that Satan may not tempt you because of your lack of self control. 1

CORINTHIANS 7: 8

To the unmarried and the widows I say that it is good for them to remain single as I am.

1 CORINTHIANS 11: 12

For as woman was made from man, so man is now born of woman. And all things are from God.

1 CORINTHIANS 7: 12 - 15

To the rest I say (I, not the Lord) that if any brother has a wife who is an unbeliever, and she consents to live with him, he should not divorce her. If any woman has a husband who is an unbeliever, and he consents to live with her, she should not divorce him. For the unbelieving husband is made holy because of his wife, and the unbelieving wife is made holy because of her husband. Otherwise your children would be unclean, but as it is, they are holy. But if the unbelieving leaves, let them leave. A brother or a sister is not under bondage in such cases. But God has called us to peace.

1 CORINTHIANS 7: 39

A wife is bound to her husband as long as he lives. But, if her husband dies, she is free to be married to whom she wishes, only in the Lord.

1 CORINTHIANS 9: 5

Do we not have the right to take along a believing wife, as do the other apostles and brothers of the Lord and Cephas?

1 CORINTHIANS 11: 3

But I want you to understand that the head of every man is CHRIST, the head of a wife is her husband, and the head of Christ is God.

EPHESIANS 5: 22 - 33

Wives, submit to your own husbands, as to the Lord. For the husband is the head of the wife even as Christ is head of the church, his body, and is himself its Savior. Now as the church submits to Christ, so also wives should submit in everything to their husbands. Husbands, love your wives, as Christ loved the church and gave himself up for her, that he might sanctify her, having cleansed her by the washing of water with the word.

EPHESIANS 5: 25 - 32

Husbands, love your wives, as Christ loved the church and gave himself up for her, that he might sanctify her, having cleansed her by the washing of water with the word, so that he might present the church to himself in splendor, without spot of, wrinkle or any such thing, that she might be holy and without blemish. In the same way husbands should love their wives as their own bodies. He who loves his wife, loves himself. For no one ever hated his own flesh, but nourishes and cherishes it, just as Christ does the church.

COLOSSIANS 3: 18

Wives, submit to your husbands, as is fitting in the Lord.

1 TIMOTHY 4: 3

Who forbid marriage and require abstinence from foods that God created to be received with thanksgiving by those who believe and know the truth.

1 TIMOTHY 3: 12

Let deacons each be the husband of one wife, managing their children and their own household as well.

1 TIMOTHY 5: 14

So I would have younger widows marry, bear children, manage their households, and give the adversary no reason for slander.

1 TIMOTHY 3: 2

Therefore an overseer must be above reproach, the husband of one wife, sober minded, self controlled, respectable, hospitable, able to teach.

HEBREWS 13: 1 - 25

Let brotherly love continue. Do not neglect to show hospitality to strangers, for thereby some have entertained angels unawares. Remember those who are in prison, as though in prison with them, and those who are mistreated, since you also are in the body. Let marriage be held in honor among all, and let the marriage bed be undefiled, for God will judge the sexually immoral and adulterous. Keep your life free from the love of money and be content with what you have, for he has said, "I will never leave you or, forsake you.

1 PETER 3: 1 - 13

Likewise, wives, be subject to your own husbands, so that even if some do not obey the word, they may be won without a word by the conduct of their wives, when they see your respectful and pure conduct. Do not let your adorning be external - the braiding of hair and the putting on of gold jewelry, or the clothing you wear - but let your adorning be the hidden person of the heart with the imperishable beauty of a gentle and quiet spirit, which in Gods sight is very precious. For this is how the holy women who hoped in God used to adorn themselves, by submitting to their own husbands.

NOTES

NOTES

NOTES

NOTES

Chapter 4

God's Promise to Abraham

For those of you that, are Bible students, I suppose you are wondering why I started here. Yes, I know that, there is a lot of valuable material before you get to this point in the Bible but, you must remember, that part of this book is how to understand the scriptures and this subject is one of the keys to it.

I have assumed, in writing this, that you already know the stories of Adam and Eve, Noah and the flood, King David and the other favorite Bible stories.

I do realize, that I have a wide variety of readers so, I have to try and not bore those who are well versed but, on the other hand, I have those who know little or nothing and that means that, I do not have a very easy job. I am taking you to the part that, I learned in the beginning of my understanding and knowing what I do now. I believe lack of having an understanding of the above subject plus Moses Law, is the backbone of all the doctrines that, man has come up with over the years and the various religious divisions.

You will find the story of Abraham if, you would like to follow along, beginning in Genesis Chapter 11.

There is no record of Abraham's youth other than, his name was Abram and God later changed his name, as we will see in the following chapters.

Abraham's father was Terah. Abraham had two brothers, Nahor and Harah. Harah had a son named Lot. This would be Abraham's nephew. Lot's father died at an early age.

Abraham's wife was Sarai, later changed to Sarah by God. Sarah and Abraham had no children. This fact will become a very important factor, as you will see in the following chapters.

Abraham, along with his father and his wife Sarah lived in the land of Ur of the Chileans, along with his nephew, Lot.

When Abraham was 75 years old, God came to him and said, "Go forth from your country and from your relatives and from your fathers house, to the land which, I will show you and I will make you a great nation and I will bless you and make your name great and so, you shall be a blessing and I will bless those who bless you and the one who curses you, I will curse. And in you, all the families of the earth shall be blessed".

So, that you will not have to try and figure this out on your own, Abraham is the beginning of the lentage that goes all the way down to Jesus and this lentage can be found in the first chapter of the book of Matthew in the New Testament. This promise to Abraham that, in him, all the families of the earth will be blessed, was talking about the coming of Jesus many years later.

So, Abraham did as the Lord had told him. Lot and Sarah went with him and they went to the land of Canaan and took all of their possessions and people that, they had acquired.

Again, the Lord appeared to Abraham and said, "To your descendants I will give this land" so, Abraham built an alter to the Lord at the place where God had appeared unto him.

At this time, there was a great famine in the land so, Abraham went to Egypt to stay for awhile and as he got close, he told Sarah to say that, she was his sister because, she was very beautiful and he was afraid that, the Egyptians would kill him when they saw her.

The ruler of Egypt was Pharaoh and some of his officials saw Sarah and told the Pharaoh about her. Sarah was taken to Pharaoh's house and Pharaoh treated Abraham very well because of her and gave Abraham sheep, oxen, donkeys, and camels along with male and female servants.

The scriptures do not say if, the Pharaoh had sex with Sarah or not, we can only assume because, God struck Pharaoh and his house with great plagues because of Sarah so, Pharaoh learned that Sarah was Abraham's wife and not his sister and Pharaoh had his men escort Abraham away.

Abraham went back to the land of Canaan where, he had originally settled between Bethel and AI. Lot and Abraham where very rich, possessing not only large amounts of gold and silver but, each had large flocks and herds. So large, that the land would not produce enough for both of their herds.

This caused great strife between the herdsmen of Lot's livestock and the herdsmen of Abraham's livestock.

Abraham was troubled by this strife, not wanting hard feelings between him and Lot so, he asked Lot which way he wanted to go and Abraham would go the other way.

Lot saw that the Valley of the Jordan was well watered and chose it so, Lot and Abraham separated from each other.

Abraham moved close to the city of Sodom and the Lord appeared again to him and told him to look as far as he could see in any direction and he would give the land to him and his descendants forever. God told him, "I will make your descendants as the dust of the earth, so that if, anyone can number the dust of the earth, then your descendants can also be numbered".

"Arise, walk about the land through its length and width for, I will give it to you".

Sometime later, Lot was living in Sodom and the city was attacked and Lot was taken captive. When word reached Abraham, he led a force of three hundred eighteen (318) trained men in pursuit.

Abraham and his men defeated King Chedorlaomer and the kings that were with him and brought back Lot, along with the people of Sodom that were taken captive and also, all their goods. They were met by the King of Sodom and Melchizedek, a priest of God who, wanted to give Abraham a tenth of everything, but Abraham would not accept anything but, allowed some of his men to accept it.

The Lord came to Abraham in a vision and said, "Do not fear, I am a shield to you, your reward shall be very great."

Since, Abraham and Sarah had no children, someone born in their house stood to be Abraham's heir; this was an important issue with him.

Abraham replied to God, "O Lord God, what would you give me, since I am childless and the heir of my house is Elizer of Damascus? Since, you have given no offspring to me; one born in my house is my heir". The Lord replied, "this man will not be your heir, but, one who shall come from your own body, he should be your heir".

The Lord took Abraham outside and said, "Now look towards the heavens and count the stars, if, you are able to count them, so shall your descendants be."

So, Abraham believed the Lord and the Lord said to him, "I am the Lord who brought you out of Ur of the Chaldeans, to give you this land, to posses it." Abraham replied, "O Lord God, how may I know that I shall posses it?" So, God said, "Bring me a three (3) year old heifer and a three (3) year old female goat and a three (3) year old ram and a turtle dove and a young pigeon".

When he did as the Lord had said, he cut them into except, for the birds and laid each half opposite of the other and as the sun went down, the Bible says, a great terror of darkness came over Abraham and God said unto him, "know for certain that your descendants will be strangers in a land that is not theirs, where they will be enslaved and oppressed four hundred (400) years. But, I will also judge the nation whom they will serve and afterwards, they will come out with many possessions and as for you, you shall go to your fathers in peace and shall be buried at a good old age. Then in the fourteenth generation, they shall return here, for the iniquity of the emirate is not yet complete".

On that day, God made a covenant with Abraham saying, "To your descendants I have given this land, from the river of Egypt as far as the Euphrates River".

The land that was spoken of here of course, was the land of Canaan where Abraham was now dwelling but, more importantly, God foretold that the descendants of Abraham or, the Hebrew people which, is referred to as Israelites being enslaved by the Egyptians for four hundred (400) years. This is where Moses comes in later on.

Abraham and Sarah were still without children and now in their eighties. Sarah, knowing how badly Abraham wanted children, offered her Egyptian maid to him as his wife. Problems arose, however, after

Sarah's maid Hagar, became pregnant. Hagar began to despite Sarah so, Sarah went to Abraham about it but, he told her to do what she wanted to with Hagar since, Hagar belonged to her. So, Sarah began to treat Hagar very harshly.

This caused Hagar to run away and was at a spring of water in the wilderness on the way to Shur when; an angel of the Lord came to her and told her to return to Sarah and submit herself to Sarah's authority.

The angel said, "I will greatly multiply your descendants so that, they shall be too many to count. Behold, you are with child and you shall bare a son and you shall call his name Ishmael, because the Lord has given to your affliction. He will be a wild donkey of a man, his hand will be against everyone and everyone's hand will be against him and he will live to the east of all his brothers".

Abraham was eight-six (86) years old when Hagar bore a son to him. He called the son Ishmael as, the angel had said.

Now, when Abraham was ninety-nine (99) years old, the Lord appeared unto him and said, "I am God almighty, walk before me and be blameless. I will establish my covenant between me and you and I will multiply you exceedingly. As for me, behold, my covenant is with you and you shall be the father of a multitude of nations. Your name shall no longer be called Abram but, shall now be Abraham for; I will make you the father of the multitude of nations. I will make you exceedingly fruitful and I will make nations of you and kings shall come forth from you."

"I will establish my covenant between me and you and your descendants after you, throughout their generations for everlasting covenant, to be God to you and to your descendants after you."

"I will give to you and to your descendants after you, the Land of Canaan for an everlasting possession and I will be their God."

"Now, as for you, you shall keep my covenant, you and your descendants after you throughout their generations."

"This is my covenant, which you shall keep, between me and you and your descendants after you; every male among you shall be circumcised and you shall be circumcised in the flesh of your foreskin and it shall be the sign of the covenant between me and you and every male among you who, is eight days old should be circumcised throughout your generations, a servant who is born in the house or is bought with money from any foreigner, who is not of your descendants."

"A servant who, is born in your house or who, is bought with your money shall surely be circumcised, thus shall my covenant be in your flesh for an everlasting covenant but, an uncircumcised male who is not circumcised in the flesh of his foreskin shall be cut off from his people, he has broken my covenant."

This covenant is very important, in understanding the New Testament because; it is referred to many times. The practice of circumcision was still being done when Jesus came so, you may want to take a highlighter pen or pencil and mark this part for easy reference or make notes at the end of the chapter.

God then said to Abraham, "as for Sariah your wife, you shall not call her Sariah but Sarah shall be her name. I will bless her and indeed I will give you a son by her. Then, I will bless her and she shall be a mother of nations, kings of people shall come from her."

When Abraham heard this, he fell on his face and laughed because, he couldn't believe that a man one hundred (100) years old with a ninety (90) year old wife was going to have a child.

God further told him, "Sarah, your wife, shall bare you a son and you shall call his name Isaac and I will establish my covenant with him for an everlasting covenant for his descendants after him."

"As for Ishmael, I will bless him and make him fruitful and will multiply him exceedingly. He shall become the father of twelve (12) princesses' and I will make him a great nation but my covenant will be established with Isaac whom Sarah will bare to you at the season next year."

After this, Abraham took his son Ishmael and all the servants who were born in his house and all who were bought with his money, every male among his household and circumcised them all the same day as God had said to him.

Abraham was also circumcised which, was at age ninety-nine (99) and his son Ishmael was thirteen (13) at the time.

One day, the Lord appeared to him during the heat of the day while he was setting at his tent door. When Abraham lifted up his eyes, three men were standing opposite of him and when he saw them, he ran from the tent door and bowed himself to the earth and said, "My Lord if I have found favor in your sight, please do not pass me by." So, they stayed and ate with him and Abraham was told of the Lord's plans to destroy Sodom because the city was so wicked.

So, the cites of Sodom and Gomorrah were destroyed but, angels went to Lot and told him to get out of Sodom and not to look back but, Lot's wife did look back and was instantly turned into a pillar of salt.

Lot and his two (2) daughters stayed in a cave. His daughters were afraid no man would have them plus, they realized their father was old and fearful that the family name would die if, they did not have children so, and they conspired to get Lot drunk. One daughter had relations the first night and the second daughter the next night. Lot did not remember anything.

Both daughters got pregnant. The first born had a son and called his name Moab. He is beginning of the Moabites.

The second daughter also had a son and called his name Ben-ammi. He is the beginning of the sons of Ammon.

Isaac was born when Abraham was one hundred (100) years old. Sarah and Hagar, her Egyptian maid, had problems once again. Sarah did not want Ishmael to be co-heir with her son Isaac so; Abraham sent Hagar and her son away.

Ishmael lived in the wilderness and became an archer. His mother took a wife for him, from Egypt.

I want to point out that, it is not my purpose to search the scripture and merely report to you what you could go read for yourself, the purpose is, to let you see how Abraham and God's promise to him are passed down the generations and by following his descendants, you can get a clear picture of how these events, along with Moses Law, is the key to understanding God's will for man today, through the New Testament.

There are many things and events that, are left out and are not explained in detail because, they're not important in helping you make this connection so, I strongly urge you to read this on your own. Now, back to my story.

Sarah lived to be one hundred twenty-seven (127) years old and she died. After her death, Isaac married Rebecca and Abraham remarried a woman named Keturah who bore him six (6) more children. Isaac was his first born so, Abraham gave all that he had to Isaac and Abraham died at age one hundred seventy-five (175). Ishmael had twelve (12) sons and he died when he was one hundred thirty-seven (137) years old.

Isaac's wife, Rebecca had two (2) sons, Essau and Jacob when Isaac was sixty (60) years old.

Essau was Isaac's favorite and had birth rights, but one day he came in from hunting and was very thirsty and hungry and Jacob was cooking some stew and Essau wanted some badly, but Jacob made him sell his birth right to him first, in order to get the food.

God made the promise to Isaac that, he did to his father, Abraham. He also repeated the promise to Jacob later on.

Jacob married two (2) women, Leah and Rachel but loved only Rachel. The two women were sisters. Leah had four sons, Rebun, Simon, Levis and Judeth. Now, Rachel was barren so, she gave her maid Bilhah, to Jacob for a wife and so, another son was born. His name was Dan and a second son was born, named Naphtali.

In the meantime, Leah had stopped bearing so, she gave her maid, Zilpah to Jacob and another son was born and was named Gad. A second son was also born and named Asher.

Leah later had two (2) more sons, Issachar and Zebalun, along with a daughter Dinah. Rachel finally had a son. His name was Joseph. So, in all, Jacob had twelve (12) sons and a daughter and Rachel died after Benjamin's birth.

This is a very important point to remember because later, God, later on, changes Jacob's name to Israel and his twelve (12) sons and their descendants are often referred to as the twelve tribes of Israel.

After being away for twenty (20) years, living with Rachel's father, Jacob returned to Canaan where Isaac lived. Isaac died at age one hundred eighty (180). Essau moved away from Jacob to another land because, the land would not carry all of the livestock they each possessed. Essau is referred to as Edem and is the father of the Edemites.

Now, when Joseph was seventeen (17) years old, he was pasturing his flock, along with his brothers and he brought back a bad report on them to his father. Israel (Jacob) loved Joseph more than he loved all his other sons and he gave Joseph a multicolor tunic (coat).

Joseph's brothers hated him and could not speak to him on a friendly basis because; they saw that their father favored Joseph.

Things got much worse when Joseph repeated to them a dream he had because, he said that, in his dream, they were binding sheaves in the field when his sheaf rose up and stood erect and their sheaves gathered around and fell down to his sheaf. His brothers said, "Are you actually going to reign over us? Or are you really going to rule over us?" So they hated him even more.

When Joseph told it to Israel, his father rebuked him and said, "What is this dream that you have had? Shall I, your mother and brothers actually come to bow ourselves down before you to the ground?" Even so, Israel kept Joseph's dream in his mind.

This dream and others that Joseph had later came true as Joseph reached a high ranking in Pharaoh's court in the land of Egypt.

One day, Israel sent Joseph to check on his brothers who were pasturing the flock some distance away.

They saw Joseph coming from a distance, because Joseph had the multicolored tunic on and they plotted against him and so, they took the tunic from Joseph and threw him into a dry pit. They had no plans to kill him.

As they were eating, a caravan of Ishmalites came by, on their way to Egypt and was carrying spices to sale so, his brothers sold Joseph to the Ishlamites and this is how Joseph wound up in Egypt. Joseph's brothers killed a male goat and dipped the tunic into the goat's blood and took it to Israel and led him to believe a wild beast had killed Joseph.

Meanwhile, Joseph was sold to Potiphar, the captain of pharaoh's bodyguard, which was in Egypt.

Potiphar saw that God was with Joseph and blessed everything he did so, he made Joseph his personal servant and made him overseer of his house and put him in charge of all that he owned.

Joseph was a very handsome man and was desired by Potiphar's wife and so, she tried to persuade Joseph to have sex with her, but he would not do so. One day, all of the men of the household were gone when Joseph 'came in to do his work and Potiphar's wife approached him again and grabbed his garment which, evidentially, was a loose fitting outer garment and Joseph fled leaving his garment in her hand. Joseph's rejection of her made her mad at him so, she accused him of making advances to her and said that, when he did, that she screamed and he ran away and she used his garment as proof.

Joseph's master put him in prison because of this, but the Lord was with him. The Chief Jailer put Joseph in charge of all of the other prisoners so, whatever Joseph did, the Lord made it prosper.

Later, the Pharaoh of Egypt put his cup barrier and baker in jail where Joseph was and he was in charge of them.

They both had a dream and after telling both that, only God could interrupt dreams, Joseph interrupted their dreams and told the cup barrier that, this meant, in three days he we be restored to his former position and asked him to mention to Pharaoh about him being in prison.

Joseph told the baker that his dream meant that, in three days Pharaoh would hang him and the birds would eat his flesh.

Both dreams came true just as Joseph had said however, the cup barrier did not speak to the Pharaoh about Joseph as Joseph had asked him to do.

Two (2) years later though, the Pharaoh had a dream and he could not find anyone who could interrupt it for him, but the cup barrier then, remembered Joseph and told Pharaoh about him so, Joseph was brought to Pharaoh and told Pharaoh that, his dream meant that, there was going to be seven (7) years of abundance in Egypt followed by seven (7) years of famine.

Pharaoh put Joseph in charge of overseeing the storing of one fifth (1/5) of all the grain that, was harvested in each of the seven good years so, that there would be plenty of food for the people in the seven bad ones and made Joseph second in command to himself.

The famine was over the entire earth and Joseph sold the grain that was stored from the unused portions.

Now, Jacob heard that, there was grain in Egypt so, he sent Joseph's brothers down to Egypt to purchase some grain. Only Benjamin did not go. Joseph was the ruler over the land and his brothers came to him to buy the grain and bowed to him with their faces to the ground because, they did not recognize him, but Joseph knew who they were.

Joseph questioned them about, whether their father was still alive and other matters and found that they had left their youngest brother, Benjamin, at home so, Joseph really gave them a hard time, accusing them of being spies.

Joseph let all of his brothers except Simeon return to their homes, warning them that, they would not see Simon again unless, they return with their youngest brother.

All of this was told to their father Israel, (Jacob) and he refused to let Benjamin go but, when their grain that they had purchased ran out, he agreed to do so.

On their return trip, Joseph finally told them who he was and had them get their father and all their possessions along with their families and move to the land of Egypt.

During the famine Joseph gave grain to the people in exchange for their flocks and land and one year in return, they were to give back one fifth (1/5) of all they grew to Pharaoh. This remained valid for many years.

Jacob lived in Egypt for seventeen (17) years before he died at the age of one hundred fifty-seven (157) and made Joseph promise not to bury him in Egypt.

There are many interesting details that room, in this writing, will not permit but, would prove valuable if, you would take the time to read Genesis but, the point of covering the main events is that, you must understand what went on from the time of God's promise to Abraham to the coming of Jesus otherwise, you will remain lost in the religious confusion evident today so, don't let this bore you if, you already know some parts or, even all of what, I am now telling.

When I tie the New Testament in, even those of you that may be teachers or preachers will see, why I wrote the section on "Brain Washing".

Joseph lived one hundred ten (110) years and died in Egypt but, he made his brothers promise to carry him out of Egypt so, he was embalmed and placed in a coffin. We will see later on that, his coffin was carried out as Moses leads the Israelites out of Egypt.

NOTES

NOTES

NOTES

NOTES

Chapter 5

Moses' Law

In Exodus, chapter 1, you will see that, after Joseph died, a new king arose over Egypt and did not know Joseph. Over time, the Israelites had grown so much in population that, they out numbered the Egyptians.

Now, the new Pharaoh was an evil man and put the Israelites in slavery and was very unkind to them. Because the Israelites were multiplying so fast, the Pharaoh commanded that, all newborn males of the Israelites were to be thrown into the Nile River.

One day, Pharaoh's daughter went to the Nile River to take a bath and she found a baby in a wicker basket among the reeds, by the river.

This male baby had been placed there, unknown to the Pharaoh's daughter, by one of her nurses that, was a Hebrew. The daughter decided to keep the baby and so, the baby needed someone to breast feed it and so, it wound up back with his original mother but, still was unknown to Pharaoh's daughter that, this was her maids son as, her maid was an Israelite woman.

Pharaoh's daughter named this baby Moses. At this time, there had been over 400 years that, the Egyptians had the Israelites in slavery.

When Moses was grown, one day, he saw an Egyptian beating a Hebrew (Israelite). Looking to make sure no one saw him, he killed the Egyptian and hid him in the sand but, some of the Hebrews let the matter be known and when Pharaoh heard of it, he tried to kill Moses. Moses fled into another country and married and became a shepherd.

One day, an angel of the Lord appeared unto him in a blazing fire from the mist of a bush yet, the bush did not burn up.

God called to Moses from the bush, "Moses, Moses" and Moses replied, "here I am" and the Lord said, "Do not come near here, remove your sandals from your feet, for the place on which you are standing is holy ground". God went on to tell Moses that he remembered the covenant that he had made to Abraham, Isaac and Jacob and that he had seen the affection of the Israelites in Egypt.

Moses doubted his speaking ability as God had instructed him to go to Pharaoh and tell him the Lord of host says, "Let my people go".

God agreed to let Aaron, Moses' brother, go with him to see Pharaoh because, Aaron was a good spokesman.

Moses met Aaron and told him what God had said and in return, Aaron met with the elders of Israel and told them what was going on.

Moses and Aaron went to Pharaoh and told him what God had said but, Pharaoh was stubborn and would not let the people go so, God turned all the rivers, pools and all water into blood so that, all the fish died. They kept going to the Pharaoh and demanding that he let the people go and each time, the Pharaoh refused so, different plagues were sent upon Egypt as Pharaoh refused to let the people go and each time, God brought a different plague upon the land of Egypt. The second (2nd) plague was frogs everywhere, even in the houses. The third (3rd) plague was gnats. The next plague was swarms of insects but, God did not allow the people of Israel to be punished with these plagues, only the Egyptians.

Next a pestilence came upon all the livestock that caused all of them to die. Next were boils upon all the Egyptian people. Next was severe hail that destroyed all plants, crops and trees. Next, was the plague of locusts.

Pharaoh remained stubborn so, God sent the last plague which, was the killing of the entire first born of Egypt, by the angel of death, both man and beast, and it occurred about midnight.

So that the angel of death would be able to divide Israel from this plague, they were to put the blood of a lamb on the two door post on the door lintel of their homes and when the angel of death came, striking the Egyptians, he would see the blood and Passover the Israelites. This event, "Passover", was to be observed by Israel and as we read the books of Acts centuries later, we find the Jews still observing the Passover feast. This was so the Israelites people would always remember how God dealt with the Egyptians and how merciful he was to the Israelites (Exodus chapter 12).

There was not one home among the Egyptians were someone did not die as God brought his wrath upon Egypt so, Pharaoh finally agreed to let the people of Israel go.

Now, the children of Israel had been in slavery for four hundred thirty (430) years to the day when they began to depart. The time frame here is about one thousand three hundred (1300) BC. There were about six hundred thousand (600,000) men (Exodus 12:37) and counting women and children, this would be about two million (2,000,000) that left Egypt that, made up the Israelite nation.

The Passover was to be observed on the first day of that month and done on a yearly basis and further, they were to eat unleavened bread for seven (7) days.

Now, as the children of Israel were leaving and approaching the Red Sea, Pharaoh became hardened in his heart, changed his mind and sent his army after Israel.

God's presence was evident in a pillar of fire over them by night and a pillar of cloud during the day as they traveled, directing them which way to go but, in spite of this and the plagues that they saw God bring upon Egypt, they panicked when they found out that Pharaoh's army was coming after them, failing their first test of faith.

Everyone knows the story of how God instructed Moses to spread his rod over the Red Sea and the waters departed and the Israelites went across to the other side on dry ground but, when Pharaoh's army tried to follow, God caused the water to come back together and all the Egyptian army was destroyed.

They traveled from the Red Sea, but had not found water for three (3) days and the people began to grumble because, the water that they found was bitter, but God threw a tree into the water and it became sweet.

Then, on the fourteenth (14th) day of the second (2nd) month after leaving Egypt, the people complained about the lack of meat and bread and how plentiful it was in Egypt and how good they had it, as far is food is concerned, in Egypt.

The Lord sent quail into the camp by the thousands for meat and also provided bread for everyone to eat.

The people were instructed to observe the Sabbath (Saturday) which, meant that, he would provide enough food on Friday for two (2) days and that there was to be no work or gathering of food on the Sabbath as, they were instructed to rest on that day.

The bread that they were eating was called manna and was eaten for forty (40) years until they came to the border of the land of Canaan.

Once again, the people started to complain about water and God told Moses to strike a rock at Mt. Horeb with his rod that, he was given by God and when Moses struck the rock, water came out.

In the third (3rd) month after leaving Egypt, they came to Mt. Sinai. Here God brought Moses upon the mountain and met with Moses and gave the Ten Commandments to him to give to the people:

1. "You shall have no other God's before me".

2. "You shall not make for yourself an idol, or any likeness of what is in heaven above or the earth beneath or in the water under the sea. You should not worship them or serve them, for I, the Lord your God, am a jealous God, visiting the iniquity of the fathers on the children on the third (3rd) and fourth (4th) generations of those who hate me but showing love and kindness to thousand's, to those who love me and kept my commandments".

3. "You shall not take the name of the Lord your God in vain, for the Lord will not leave him unpunished who takes his name in vain".

4. "Remember the Sabbath day and keep it holy. Six (6) days you shall labor and do all your work, but the Sabbath day is a Sabbath of the Lord your God, in it you should not do any work, you or your son or your daughter, your male servant

or your female servant or your cattle or your sojourner who stays with you. For in six (6) days the Lord made the heavens and the earth, the sea and all that is in them and rested on the seventh (7th) day therefore, the Lord blessed the Sabbath and made it holy".

5. "Honor your father and your mother that your days may be prolonged in the land in which the Lord your God gives you".

6. "You shall not murder".

7. "You shall not commit adultery".

8. "You shall not steal".

9. "You shall not bare false witness against your neighbor".

10. "You shall not covet your neighbor's house; you shall not covet your neighbor's wife or his male servant or his female servant or his ox or his donkey or anything that belongs to your neighbor".

In addition to the Ten Commandments, many ordinances were given also as all can see from chapter 20-23 in the book of Exodus.

In chapter 24, God calls Moses back up on the mountain to give him the Ten Commandments on stone written by God (verse 12).

In chapter 25, God gives Moses instructions for building the sanctuary (Tabernacle). God also gave instructions for the Ark of the Covenant. This ark contains the tablets of stone that had the Ten Commandments on them.

Chapter 28, we seen Aaron and his sons were to be priests and special clothing was made for them.

I guess this is where some preachers and leaders get the entire garb that they wear today which, is just left over from this part of the Old Testament. The part that I have not figured out is, if it is out of ignorance, tradition, trying to keep part of Moses law and part of Christ or trying to make the congregation think they are somebody special but, I tend to think it is the latter.

God gave Moses two (2) tablets of stone with the Ten Commandments on them that were written by God's on finger (Chapter 31, verse 18).

Moses was on the mountain for forty (40) days and so the people got inpatient and talked Aaron into making a golden calf for them and the people made sacrifices to it and worshipped it and this angered Moses so much whenever he found out that, he threw the two (2) tablets down and shattered them.

In Chapter 34, God has Moses cut two (2) more tablets of stone and he wrote on them again and re- made the stone with the Ten Commandments on them.

As you read the rest of Exodus, you will see all kinds of instructions that God gave to Moses in regards to the making of the ark, the Tabernacle, Aaron's priestly clothing along with instructions for burnt offerings.

As I said, it was not just the Ten Commandments as some people think today, Moses Law was dozens of offerings, sacrifices, observance of special religious holidays and seasons, etc. that, were all part of this law.

There was also the law of Burnt Offering, the Grain Offering, the Sin Offering, the Guilt Offering, the Ordination Offering and the Sacrifice of Peace Offering (Read the book of Leviticus).

In order to be a priest, under Moses Law, you had to be from the tribe of Levi and you had to be a direct descendent of Aaron. This shows the so-called priest of today for what they are-fakes! Why? Because all the Jewish records of descendants were destroyed when the Roman army attacked Jerusalem in about AD 70 so, no one knows if, they are a relative to Aaron or not so therefore cannot be a priest. Secondly, we have a high priest in Jesus and do not need another one.

There were twelve (12) tribes or in other words, descendants of Jacob (remember Jacob's name was changed to Israel) and he had twelve (12) sons so, over the years, the descendants grew greatly in numbers. The names of Israel's (Jacob's sons) are listed in the book of Numbers, Chapter 1, Verses 5-15.

The main thing that, I want you to understand about Moses Law is, it was given to Israel and no one else so, simply put, unless you were a Jew and if, the law was still effective today, most would be a gentile. You will see in the New Testament that, the gentiles were, "without God in the world". In other words, Moses Law would not apply to you if, you were a gentile. The gentiles had no hope until Jesus came.

You would also have a problem in proving you are a Jew because, as I said, all the records were destroyed when the Roman army attacked in AD 70 and the high priest of the tribe of Levi kept all these records so, a Jew cannot prove he is a Jew in this day and time because, they cant trace their family tree back to Abraham.

The Law of Moses was to last until the seed (Christ) came and at his death, he nailed it to his cross (Colossians 2:14).

I could cover a lot more about the numerous laws, feasts, etc. that, is involved in Moses Law which, reminds me, some people or groups today attempt to keep parts of Moses Law but, that won't work. The Apostle Paul said if, you mess up on one point, you've broken the whole law so, you must keep all of it or none and no one could keep the law perfectly and that is why Jesus had to die because, as the book of Hebrews states, "the blood of bulls and goats could not take away sin." Only the blood of Jesus could take away sin so, as the Apostle Paul states in the New Testament if, we are under law, that is, a system of law keeping (Moses Law) then, Jesus died for nothing.

NOTES

NOTES

NOTES

NOTES

Chapter 6

Handling Objections

Homosexuals talk a lot about love. Of course any two (2) people have a right to love each other. However, this isn't about love, it's about sinful sexual perversion. I have a right to love my sister. I don't have a right to pursue her sexually even if, she consents. That's how disgusting homosexuality really is. According to homosexuals, as long as sex is between two (2) adults (over age 18) and both agree then, we should leave them alone. With that reasoning then, a father who lusts after his own daughter and wants sex with her and she is over age eighteen (18) and she agrees, it's ok. That's sick. This is how bad some people are messed up in the head.

One of the main things people are overlooking is, these people are committing fornication. Fornication is sexual intercourse between two (2) people who aren't married to each other. I suppose, to be truthful about it, most non homosexuals do that all the time however, it doesn't change the fact that fornicators are on Paul's and Peters list of sins people commit and practice sinning that definitely won't make it to heaven.

A person cannot be a homosexual and justify it by the bible. Some try and fall on their face. Others justification is to just deny God and the Bible. So that you can have the knowledge of the care given in the passing down of manuscripts in many different languages over many centuries, below, I am including that so, homosexuals cannot use your bible ignorance against you (I mean that in a good way).

Since, it has been more than twenty (20) years, it is, to some degree, very difficult to remember exactly, step by step, how I obtained my knowledge in understanding the scripture but, I do recall thinking it was like a jigsaw puzzle and wondered how in the world anyone could figure all this out. I did figure it out and I can tell you that next to the Bible, this will be the most eye-opening religious material that you have ever read, whether, you are a new creature in Christ or, you are a seasoned Minister.

First, there has to be basis of authority and that is the Bible. Anymore than the Bible is too much and anything less than Bible is not enough!

I am not interested in any man made doctrines or commandments of mere men nor, am I interested in using or studying with a "Bible" that was written and translated by one man such as the Living Bible. There are many denominations that, have their little creed books that, are filled with man-made doctrines. They are too much.

Which Bible? I don't want anything to do with one man's version of a translation as, I said above. I have never seen one that did not conform to that one person's closed minded thinking so, this is too much.

I suggest that, you find one that is easy to read (in today's language) so, you can easily have a clear understanding of what is being said.

Next, find a dependable translation. This means that, several biblical scholars, not just one man, translated that particular version, lowering the chance for error.

Personally, I started with the King James Version but, it is very difficult to understand for the beginner so, I recommend the New King James Version which, is in today's language or, the New International Version which, is also in today's language.

In case you don't know, the Old Testament was written in Hebrew and the New Testament was written in Greek. It was the Greek that caused all the translation problems.

What I mean by problems is, there are words in the Greek that do not mean what we mean in English. For instance, the Greek word for love has one meaning in English but, that same word in Greek has several so, a misapplication or mistranslation could change what the original writer meant completely.

Why am I telling you all of this? Because, if, only one person or three or four people translate the Greek into the English, there is a lot of room for error. This is greatly reduced when, many scholars get together to translate the scripture. Previously, I had mentioned my distaste with the Living Bible because; it was written and translated by only one man. As a for instance, in one place where the original Greek says, "we are saved by faith", he added the word "only". Changing that one word made all the difference in the world, in what was originally meant because, we are saved by a combination of a lot things, i.e., grace, works, faith, baptism, believing, etc. By no means, are we saved by any one of these standing alone, in and of itself.

In comparison, the King James Version was translated by over fifty (50) Greek scholars, the American Standard Version by over one hundred (100) Greek scholars and the New International Version was translated by over two hundred (200) scholars.

Are there mistakes in every version? You better believe it! Many religious minded people especially, the senior citizens group, are very naive to this fact and refuse to believe "old reliable", the King James Version, has these flaws. Well, surprise, surprise, it has many flaws. For example, the Greek word that was translated "Passover" was correctly translated Passover more than fifty (50) times but, the same Greek word was translated one time as, "Easter" and that one mistake has changed, possibly forever, the way the world views that day, all because of one little word change. Now are you beginning to see what I mean?

If, that's true, how can we trust anything that has been translated? Can we depend on our translations when knowing God's will, may depend on where we spend eternity?

The answer is a firm yes and the assurance of this, will be covered in detail so that, you will not wonder anymore.

A large portion of this book will be spent on the New Testament, but the Old Testament is not free from translation errors either and problems of meanings of words in changing from Hebrew to English. For example, Solomon wrote, "he that spares the rod hates the child" the word hate here, means to "love less" so, that helps us more clearly understand that passage.

In addition to having a reliable translation, I strongly suggest that every person who seeks the truth and wants to search out the scriptures on their own, from time to time, purchase a Bible concordance.

A concordance lists the words of the Bible and every scripture where, that word is located. It is extremely useful in ones study and I personally, would not try to study without it. I would suggest that you either purchase a Young's or Strong's concordance.

I suggest also that, you purchase Vine's Expository Dictionary of New Testament words which, gives the meaning of Bible words.

There are many other study materials that you would find useful if, you visited a Bible bookstore but, as time goes on and your understanding of the scripture becomes clearer, I might suggest that later on, you add an optional Greek text. These usually show the Greek word on one side with the English translation on the other.

Now, do not begin to get afraid, I'm not going to get over your head in this book as a matter of fact, most of it is plain common sense.

To those who feel that, I am talking with a double tongue, no, you do not need more than the Bible. The concordance and the Greek dictionary are simply aids that, I have listed above and are just that, aids and not an addition to the scripture. An addition is when, someone adds more to the scriptures, i.e., man-made doctrines, commandments of men, etc. in teaching others.

In writing this book, needless to say, I have my opinion on many biblical subjects but, I will do my best to stick strictly with the facts.

I think the next step in helping one to unravel all the maze of trying to understand the Bible is, to have a clear belief in the soundness of the book that we call the Bible.

Where did it come from? Can we be sure that we can trust the translations today? That is part of what this book is all about.

Let's start by clearly proclaiming that the Bible was written to be intelligible to ordinary, average people.

How do we know that we have God's word or better still, all of it since, it was a practice of the Hebrews to destroy old manuscripts once, they had written a new copy from them?

Most of you, I'm sure, have, at least, heard of the discovery of the Dead Sea scrolls by a Sheppard in 1947. He found these scrolls in a cave by accident and these are known in religious circles as the Qumran Library.

Before the Dead Sea scrolls, the earliest manuscript that we possessed was the "Massoretic Text", dating back to A.D. 500.

The evidence from these early manuscripts is invaluable in confirming the care involved in preserving the scripture.

In addition, we have the Greek version of the Old Testament, referred to as, The Septuagint (LXX). This version was used by the Greek speaking Jews in the first century.

It is uncertain how this version came about but, we can date it back to the time of Ptolemy Philadelphus of Egypt (285-246 B.C.).

As the message of Christianity spread to other parts of the world where Greek was not spoken, translations were made into Egyptian, Latin and Syriac.

The formation of the Old Testament is difficult to establish but, we can and do know what the Old Testament contained during the time period prior to the first century assembly.

We have the work of a first century A.D. historian named Josephus in which, he acknowledges twenty-two (22) books. In about 100 A.D., the Apocalypse of Esra list twenty-four (24) books. Now, if, Joecphus included the book of Ruth with judges and Lamentations with Jeremiah, then the two (2) would agree. This is a strong possibility.

The Hebrew Canon of 24 books are equal to the thirty-nine (39) books of the Greek Canon since, in the Hebrew, the books of Samuel, Kings, Chronicles, Isaiah and Neimah and along with the twelve (12) minor prophets counted as only one (1) book.

In the New Testament, most of the books of the Old Testament are quoted which, leads us to believe the Old Testament text that we have today, is the same one used by Jesus and the early Christians.

We possess thousands of the New Testament manuscripts, written in many different languages.

The council of the assembly of Laodica (AD 363) agreed on the New Testament that we have today, except, for the book of Revelation.

The council at Carthage in AD 397 also agreed with the earlier one at Laodica except, for Revelation.

The Latin vulgate was the official Version used by the assembly during the middle ages to after the reformation period when, Martin Luther produced his German version. There were also translations during this time into other European languages.

So, that I do not throw you off, this would be a good place to point out one of the other flaws in the King James Version where we commonly use the word "Church", but, maybe to your surprise, the word "Church" is not in the original text. The correct word should be Assembly. Yes, I know, thousands of people including Preachers do not know this. If, you got a Greek dictionary then, you'll find out that what I just said was true.

It was a man named Tyndale who was the first person to print the New Testament into the English language. Cloverdale published the first full Bible in the year 1553.

"The King James Version" followed in the year 1611. "The New Testament in Modern Speech" followed in the year 1903 by R. T. Weymouth, "A New Translation of the Bible" by James Moffatt was published in the year 1913 and 1924 "The Complete Bible; and American Translation" by E. J. Goodspeed in the year 1927, "The Holy Bible" by Ronald Knox in 1944 and 1949 (Roman Catholic Version based on the Latin vulgate), "The Revised Standard Version" in 1946 and 1952 by a committee of thirty-two (32) scholars, "The New World Translation" in 1950 and 1960 by the Johovah Witness group, with their interpretation of certain texts, "Authentic New Testament" by H. J. Schonfield, a Jewish scholar, "The Amplified Bible" in 1958, the work of twelve (12) men that gives different possible meanings to different words, "The New Testament in Modern English" by J. B. Phillips in 1958, in 1959, "The Holy Bible; the Burkley version in Modern English", where the Old Testament was the work of twenty (20) scholars and the New Testament was done by one (1) individual, "The New English Bible" in 1961 and 1970 sponsored by British churches, in 1966, "The Jerusalem Bible", an accurate translation of the Roman Catholic School of Biblical studies, in 1966, "Today's English Version" by the American Bible Society and in 1971, "The Living Bible" by Kenneth Taylor.

I could write dozens of pages on this subject alone but, remember, this is supposed to be an easy to read, easy to understand book.

This book is intended to give you the basics only. Who knows, I may include more controversial and complicated subjects in a later version of the book.

The Old Testament was written in the Hebrew language, the New Testament in Greek and later translated in to Latin and then to English and if, I trace this back for you it will only mess with your mind. I only intend to give you the basics-besides, I would only tend to confuse you, more than likely.

One of homosexuals' objections about the bible is, "Jesus didn't say anything about homosexuals." So? What has that fact got to do with anything? Jesus didn't have to say anything because, his father had a lot to say and God said he found it extremely disgusting and compared homosexuality to bestiality. As, we have previously seen, the practice of homosexuality is condemned in several places. I will say again, for a homosexual to try to use the bible to condone his/her homosexuality is, wasting their time. It can't be done.

Torah scrolls were copied by hand so, they were very valuable. They took care to not wear out the parchment or smudging the text by using what was called, a Torah pointer. It was most often made out of wood but, sometimes, it was made of sterling silver so, the person reading it did not have to touch the manuscript with their hands.

NOTES

NOTES

NOTES

NOTES

Chapter 7

God's Love and God's Wrath

For God so loved the world that he gave his only begotten son that whosoever believes in him shall not perish but, have everlasting life." There is much more to being saved than just believing in him for, "The devils believe also and tremble." God is simple. Either obey him or, hell will be your home. Homosexuals say it's all about love and God wouldn't do that. Gods answer to that is, "He that says he loves God and keeps not his commandments is a liar and the truth is not in him."

Homosexuals generally don't have a clue about Gods nature. Sure, he loves us and doesn't want anyone to perish. God is kind, thoughtful, considerate, caring, loving, etc however, want to anger him? All you have to do is, sin, especially sexual sins.

Nothing irks me more than someone who hasn't spent any time actually studying the Bible and have only picked up a little knowledge from mom and dad or, a Preacher from time to time and with no more than that, try to debate the Bible with those of us who have taken the time to study and learn and are dead serious about making it to Heaven. For instance, I have run across several people who refuse to believe God will send them to hell and believe God is all about forgiveness and love.

When I hear things like this, it is clear those who say things like this, knows exactly nothing about Gods nature and even less about the Bible. If you haven't really studied then, you don't know what you are talking about so, don't waste my time trying to justify your sins. Again,

I have heard many that refuse to believe they should fear God. Oh really? "Let us hear the conclusion of the whole matter the whole duty of man is to fear God and keep his commandments for this is mans all." Ecclesiastes 12:13. Did you get that? Fearing God and doing what he says is what we are all about as humans. Some carry this false thinking over to raising their children. Love and fear goes hand in hand. The police are there to help us, not write us tickets or, club us and throw us in jail. I have never been in jail nor, had a ticket for anything. Why? Because my parents taught me to respect authority. If I didn't, I would suffer the end results. If people didn't fear what the law of the land will do to them if they do things they shouldn't, we would all have to have bars over our doors and windows and all carry guns to protect ourselves.

I can spot a child in a second out in the public who has no fear of their parent(s). You have seen them. They are the ones throwing a temper tantrum because they didn't get their way. When I was a kid, I didn't have the option of acting like that unless I had an urge to get my butt spanked. They are the kids you see running all over a restaurant while their parents are ignoring them and they are disturbing everyone's night out. There are some hot shot experts who have some people believing that spanking a child will make them violent. Bologna. By the way, when I say spanking, I mean a spanking, not a beating and child abuse. Now days, spanking can almost be out of consideration as, you can make kids do about anything by taking away their cell phone. Ha. Fear of you doing that helps keep children from doing things they shouldn't. At the same time, your child knows you love them by your actions toward them. I didn't have to spank my two girls very much but, their fear of me doing so, helped to keep them on the right path. Sure, I believed in spanking as a last option.

Some think that spanking is something you do to a child and that its mean. The Bible tells you exactly how to raise your child. King Solomon was told by God that he would be the wisest (not smartest) man that had ever lived or, would ever live and so, King Solomon had several things to say about raising children and they all are just the opposite of the so called experts that claim spanking causes violence. For me, I am going to do what the wisest man to ever live has to say.

Just how strict is God about doing exactly what he says? A lot more than most people want to believe. That's because they haven't studied. God warns us how strict he is. God is about love. He gave his only son to die a miserable earthly death so, we could be saved yet, few take advantage of the world's greatest gift. Few take advantage of the greatest gift in the history of the world and instead, engage in their own lusts, having loved this world's pleasures for a short time rather than to make sure they have a home in heaven with God.

We can't say he didn't warn us. In Proverbs 30: 5-6, it is written, "Every word of God is pure. He is a shield to those who put their trust in him. Do not add to his words, least He rebuke you and you be found a liar." In the last book of the bible, the book of Revelation, he warns us again, Revelation 22:18 "For I testify to everyone who hears the words of the Prophecy of this book: If anyone adds to these things, God will add to him the plagues that are written in this book and if anyone takes away from the words of the book of this prophecy, God shall take away his part from the Book of Life, from the holy city and from the things which are written in this book.: Still think God is all about love? Yes he is but, it's conditional. You have to first obey him. He just told you what will happen to you if, you don't do what he says. He also explains how he is by giving us examples of what he did to those who didn't do exactly what he said. One is the story of Nadab & Abihu, two sons of Aaron who helped with the temple and other matters. This is a most interesting story in that it clearly shows just meaning well isn't good enough, doing exactly what God says is what matters.

The following is a good example of how strict God is and shows he means it when he says to not add anything to what he says. In this case, most of us would think what Aaron's sons did was just something minor but, God didn't think so. Remember, under Moses law, Aaron was the high Priest and his sons helped out. LEVITICUS:10 1-3 Nadab and Abihu, two sons of Aaron, each took his censer and put fire in it, put incense on it and offered strange fire before the Lord, which He had not commanded them so, fire went out from the Lord and it devoured them, and they died before the Lord and Aaron And Moses said to Aaron, "This is what the Lord spoke saying "By those who come near

WHY GOD DID NOT MAKE ANYONE HOMOSEXUAL

Me, I must be regarded as holy: and before all the people I must be glorified." so, Aaron held his peace.

In 2 SAMUEL Chapter 6, is the story of King David transporting the Ark of God to the temple. A servant, Uzzah, was walking along side an ox cart that was being used to carry the Ark when, one of the oxen stumbled (some versions say one of the wheels went upon a rock) and thinking the Ark was going to tilt over, meant well and reached up his hand and touched the Ark. God dropped him dead right there. God had said not to touch it. He meant it. Many of us have good intentions sometimes however a complete study of the bible will teach us that our salvation is dependent on our obedience in keeping his commandments. Yes, I understand grace. I am talking about those who practice certain sins. In case you don't know, the Ark of God contained the Ten Commandments that was written with Gods own finger in stone. The Ark had short arms on each side with holes to run a wood pole through and the Ark was carried by those wood poles so that no one touched the Ark.

Throughout the whole bible, God is consistent with his anger against those who sin as also shown in the New Testament where in Acts chapter 5 is the story of Ananias and his wife, Sapphira. They sold some land but, lead the congregation and Peter to believe they gave it all to the church when, in fact, they held back some of the money for themselves. Peter dropped Ananias dead in front of all the congregation. Sapphira came in later, not knowing her husband was dead and also lied and Peter dropped her dead also.

If you were really a bible student, you would find that yes, God loves us. He allowed the killing of his only son to save us from our sins but, on the other hand, salvation is dependent upon us not practicing sinning and us obeying his commandments. Of course we as Christians, will sin. That's where Gods grace through Jesus Christ comes in. We are covered by Jesus blood however, if we make it a habit of continued sinning, Peter and Paul gives us a list of those sinners who definitely aren't going to make heaven.

In 2 PETER 2: 20 - 22, Peter talks about those who became Christians then, fell away and returned to their old sinful ways and says it would have been better they had never known righteousness because their second state is now worse than the first. Jesus, in the book of Revelation the Lord told the church at Laodicea, chapter 3: 14-20 and he talks about those that have one foot in the church door and one foot out and are luke warm and says those type makes him sick to his stomach. Folks, you can't serve Christ and serve the devil at the same time. The only exception listed is, if one married mate is a Christian and their mate isn't then, the believing mate will save their unbelieving mate 1 Cor. 7: 14 - 15. No matter how well intended one is, the bible clearly teaches that if we practice sinning then, we definitely aren't going to make it to heaven.

In case you don't know, the bible not only condemns homosexuals, it condemns cross dressers: "Know you not that the unrighteous shall not inherit the kingdom of God? Don't be deceived; neither fornicators, nor idolaters, nor adulterers, nor the effeminate (cross dressers) nor abusers of themselves with mankind (homosexuals), nor thieves, nor covetous, nor drunkards, nor revilers, nor extortionist, shall inherit the kingdom of God." 1 Corinthians 6: 9-10

NOTES

NOTES

NOTES

NOTES

Chapter 8

Conclusion

What God had to say about how disgusting homosexuals are to him, is very clear. It is very clear that homosexuals were not born that way and simply messed up in the head. Homosexuals will argue that there wasn't a word in the Greek to be translated, homosexual.

First, in the translation of several versions we have today, hundreds of Greek scholars disagree. By the way, in case I haven't told you, no homosexual can prove they were born that way. Second, let's say homosexuals are correct in that there isn't a Greek word that can be translated into English. One would have to have a lot of help to misunderstand what the scripture is talking about in Romans chapter 1:24-28 "Wherefore God also gave them up to uncleanness through the lusts of their own hearts (mind) to dishonor their own bodies between themselves: Who changed the truth into a lie, and served the creature more than the Creator, who is blessed forever. Amen. For this reason God gave them up into vile affections: even their women did change the natural use (of their Vagina) into that which is against nature (being a Lesbian). and likewise, the men, leaving the natural use of the woman (trading a vagina for a rectum), burned in their lust one toward another men with men working that which is unseemly, and receiving in themselves that recompence of their error which was meet and even as they did not like to retain God in their knowledge, God gave them over to a reprobate mind (Told you they were messed up in the head) to do those things which are not convenient."

A lot of homosexuals act like and talk like the New Testament doesn't say anything about them. You just saw that's not true. Romans chapter 1 is only a starter as, you can see from the list in the second chapter. Hopefully, I educated you enough to watch out for those who just throw a scripture out at you here and there when, fact is, they know very little about the bibles teaching on the subject of homosexuality. I have heard and read about homosexuals who try to tie food eaten under Moses law or, slavery and other things as justification for their perverted ways. This is why I educated you about Moses law and the fact that Moses law was given to the Jews, no one else so, even if the homosexuals were correct, Moses law would not apply to anyone who is a non Jew, even if Moses law was still valid.

If a homosexual throws any scripture at you that has anything to do with slavery or, eating certain foods, this should tell you immediately that person doesn't know any more about the Bible than you do if, you are the average, unlearned person and he or she is just repeating something other homosexuals try to use, to no avail to better their position. Mainly, it doesn't matter what they say because, I showed you in chapter two what God thinks of homosexuals and so, whatever they have to say doesn't void what God thinks and he thinks homosexuals are comparable to a son wanting his own mother or, a beast and finds them very disgusting - and you should also when you stop and think about the perverted, disgusting acts they are doing to each other.

Lawmakers, do you care where you spend eternity? Homosexuals act against nature and are no better than any perverted child molester or, any other sex act that is a crime against nature. The Supreme Court allows you to make homosexuality a crime - and it is a crime against nature. God allowed you to be a lawmaker for a reason so, isn't it about time you and other lawmakers made homosexuality a crime? Oh sure, homosexuals are going to call you names such as bigot. You are a bigot only if your position is unfair.

This isn't about hate nor, discrimination as they will surely yell, it's about sexual perversion. I don't hate any child molester but, God tells me to avoid such people. They have the option of repenting. I sure don't want any sexual pervert to have equal standing as, who would want equality for any man and his mother who engaged in sexual perversion? Same identical thing. This is all about being extremely disgusted at homosexuals just as I would any person who would want a beast or, their own parent. That's a sickening thought. I sure wouldn't want to be in any lawmakers shoes when the day comes they have to answer to God if, they just sat back and did nothing so, they can remain popular. Woe unto you.

God loved humanity so much that he sent his only son to die for our sins. God doesn't wish that anyone should parish. If we say we love God yet, do not obey his commandments, we are a liar. Just having good intentions doesn't cut it with God if actions of obedience doesn't match our words. Would God throw one of his children down to hell? No he wouldn't. The question becomes, who is a child of God according to biblical definition? There is no middle ground. One is either a child of God or, a child of the devil. "In this, the children of God are made known and so are the children of the devil: whosoever doesn't do righteousness is not of God, neither is he that hates his brother." 1 John 3:10.

According to bible teaching, homosexuals are clearly children of the devil and we are told to avoid them. I hope I have opened your eyes to the reality of these disgusting people, no matter how they may appear to be in daily life. Obey God and love your fellow man and you will have a home in heaven.

Lawmakers and public officials, homosexuality is worse than a child molester, a peeping Tom, incest or, any other sexual perversion. It's a crime against nature and it's past time to call a spade, a spade and make it a crime against nature as it surely is.

In proof reading my book, I have come to realize all the flack I will get about what I said about getting a degree. I certainly am not against getting an education. In this time, it's absolutely necessary otherwise, be stuck with the low paying jobs. I am not against getting a degree either. I do believe rather than spend all that money and time, many should learn a trade. The problem with getting and not getting a degree is, Americans save less than any other free world country. Students are not taught about compound interest and how it works. Banks and Insurance companies surely understand. Did you know that setting aside just thirty dollars ($30.00) per month from age twenty five (25) to age forty five (45) in a good performing mutual fund (one with a proven ten (10) year or, more track record), they would have around eight hundred thousand dollars ($800,000.00)? Did you know that a one time deposit of two thousand dollars ($2,000.00) at age twenty five (25) and never add one cent to it will result in about the same amount of money. You spend much more than this eating out each week. Secure your future by educating yourself about how money works, how compound interest works, how mutual funds work and secure your retirement starting right now.

A couple of other things. One, it is common among homosexuals these days to preach tolerance. Sounds good. Even the President has bought this lie and changed his mind about homosexuality. That fact tells me real quick, like most others, the President knows very little about what the bible has to say about homosexuals. "If a man lies with a male as he lies with a woman, both of them have committed an abomination. They shall surely be put to death." Leviticus 20: 13. That's how much tolerance God has for homosexuals. I want to say to Ministers, Preachers, Church leaders, etc, if you didn't know what God has to say about the disgusting sin of homosexuality, now you do after reading this book. Every member of your church needs to know the truth about homosexuality. It is your duty as a man of God to stand up for what is right and for the truth. Woe unto you if, you don't.

NOTES

NOTES

NOTES

NOTES

Printed in the United States
By Bookmasters